T0171716

# STOPPING
## AND
# SEEING

## ALLYN RICHERT

WESTBOW
PRESS®
A DIVISION OF THOMAS NELSON
& ZONDERVAN

This book is a work of non-fiction. Unless otherwise noted, the author and the publisher make no explicit guarantees as to the accuracy of the information contained in this book and in some cases, names of people and places have been altered to protect their privacy.

WestBow Press books may be ordered through booksellers or by contacting:

WestBow Press
A Division of Thomas Nelson & Zondervan
1663 Liberty Drive
Bloomington, IN 47403
www.westbowpress.com
844-714-3454

Because of the dynamic nature of the Internet, any web addresses or links contained in this book may have changed since publication and may no longer be valid. The views expressed in this work are solely those of the author and do not necessarily reflect the views of the publisher, and the publisher hereby disclaims any responsibility for them.

Any people depicted in stock imagery provided by Getty Images are models, and such images are being used for illustrative purposes only.
Certain stock imagery © Getty Images.

Scripture quotations marked KJV are taken from the King James Version

Scripture quotations marked NIV are taken from The Holy Bible, New International Version®, NIV® Copyright © 1973, 1978, 1984, 2011 by Biblica, Inc.® Used by permission. All rights reserved worldwide.

Scripture quotations marked ESV taken from The Holy Bible, English Standard Version® (ESV®), Copyright © 2001 by Crossway, a publishing ministry of Good News Publishers. All rights reserved.

Scripture quotations marked NKJV are taken from the New King James Version®. Copyright © 1982 by Thomas Nelson. Used by permission. All rights reserved.

ISBN: 979-8-3850-1727-0 (sc)
ISBN: 979-8-3850-1728-7 (e)

Library of Congress Control Number: 2024901220

Print information available on the last page.

WestBow Press rev. date:  01/30/2024

# PREFACE

Our words are written to convey an Intended Meaning. If correctly spoken or written, You Are Led from a correct initial Understanding of a word To Expanded Meanings Inherent In The Words.

The difference between a word describing a physical reality and a word describing a Spiritual Reality Is so significant, I Will Usually Capitalize The First letter Of A Word Describing A Spiritual Reality To Distinguish It from a word with the same spelling describing a physical reality, in the context of Our Use Of The word. Also, I will not capitalize a negative spiritual word.

Another important distinction is the difference between physical "energy" and Divine or Spiritual "Energy." These Energies Are Fundamentally Different because Their Source Is From entirely different Membrane Systems. Physical "energy" is essential to physical existence in a physical universe. Divine "Energy," Manifested As Spiritual Energy, Originates Directly From GOD and Is Manifested In A Spiritual Universe. Of course, The Reality That You and I Live In, Is A temporary Fusion Of Our Spiritual Universe and our physical universe, As It May Please The LORD.

Research notes and credits are provided at the end of this Teaching. This is both, To Credit The Original Thinkers for Their Contributions Referred To and To Expand On The Truth.

If This Teaching Helps Your Spiritual Journey, You May Find Broader Inspiration Learning From This Author's Definitive Teaching, *GOD – The Dimensional Revelation.*

# 1

# SPIRITUAL ENLIGHTENMENT

When the Seeker Becomes The Light, It is Attained.[1a]

Spiritual Enlightenment is a State Of Being, Eternal, In The Present, With GOD. You Will Experience It as "I AM." This Is Your Soul Participating In The Great, "I AM"[1b] That Is GOD.

"I Am" Is Manifested In This Life As Your Consciousness. It Is Supported By The Continuums of physical and Spiritual Reality.

Participate With Stopping and Seeing, As One Way To Unify With GOD.

# 2

## STOPPING

It is difficult for a Human Being, Alive, In this world, To Advance Beyond ordinary consciousness in our physical universe. The conditioning of physical being often dominates Your Awareness, confining you to physical situations. The processes of metabolism, reproduction, survival, and ordinary perception fill your consciousness. This leaves little room for Appreciation Of Your Complete Being. Your Being Is Both a physical being and a Spiritual Being, In This Life.

You look to others for Leadership regarding what is Precious and how to Live Your Life. You Trust Their Wisdom, but You are often misled. Everyone Is In Their Own Process Of Spiritual Growth. The Spiritual Universe Is Expansive, so Each Spiritual Being Is At A Stage Of Development That May Be Very Different From The Stage Of Your Spiritual Development. Some are not growing spiritually. Many are just existing, like a leaf blown by the wind.

You Must Lead Yourself If You Seek More Meaningful Consciousness.

So - STOP! [2a]

Stop the incessant chatter in your mind.
The LORD Said, "Peace, Be Still." [2b]

# 3

# SEEING

Then SEE.

See The Perfection. Ours is not a perfect reality. Perfection is GOD's Presence In It.

See With The Eyes Of GOD.

Participate In what Your senses are Perceiving, but Sense Those Things As GOD Is Sensing Them Through You.

Yes, You Are The Instrument That GOD Uses to Participate In This World. Use Your eyes To See As GOD's Eyes. Invite GOD To Hear What You Are Hearing. Then "Seeing" Happens!

GOD Is Taking Pleasure In His Created Reality Through Your Consciousness. This Is The Reason For Your Being. It Answers The Question, "Why Am I Here?"

In fact, Your Consciousness Is The Manifestation of The Divine Spirit That Is You. GOD Is In You.[3a] Your Soul Is A Sliver Of GOD, Incarnated Into physical being, which is your body.

Jesus Said: "At that day ye shall know that I am in my Father, and ye in me, and I in you.". (*John 14:20 KJV*)

Your Highest Purpose is to Welcome GOD Into Your Consciousness. [3b] This Is The Most Sublime Meditation. Whether It

Be The Sudden Appreciation Of a physical scene, the Lovely Flow Of Music, The Rich Taste Of A Feast, The Full Aroma Of The Flower, or The Exciting Touch Of A Lover. If You Welcome GOD Into Your Sensations, The LORD Will Join You. Then You Can Join GOD In Sharing This Glory. This Is Most Fulfilling.

Jesus Said: "There is one body and one Spirit, just as you were called to one hope when you were called; one Lord, one faith, one baptism; one God and Father of all, who is over all and through all and in all." (*Holy Bible, Ephesians 4:4-6 NIV*)

Jesus Said: "If anyone loves me, he will keep my word, and my Father will love him, and we will come to him and make our home with him." (*Holy Bible, John 14;23 ESV*)

# 4

## PURITY OF MIND

Your Mind Processes Your Consciousness, As A Fusion Of your physical brain with Your Divine Spirit, also called Your Soul.

Your Immortal Soul Enters Your physical body at The Moment Of Incarnation. Your Immortal Soul Selects your body In Harmony With The Will Of GOD.

Your Soul Comes Into your body, Informed According To Your Spiritual Journey, So Far. That Information Provides The Basis For Spiritual Growth during Your Life In Your body. This Life Is A Fresh Start As Your Soul Seeks Reunification With the ONE, LORD, GOD Of All.

Now You Have The Opportunity To Become Pure In Your Consciousness.

Ordinary cognitive thinking is not Seeing. There is plenty of time in this Life for material activity, planning, and construction. Ordinary cognitive reasoning may distract you from Seeing.

If you simply Let Your brain clear its processes for a Moment, Surely You Will Attain Purity Of Mind. Then Stopping Will Occur.

Then See With The Eyes Of GOD.

# 5

## SEE WITH THE EYES OF GOD

When You See This World With The Eyes Of GOD, It Is GOD's Consciousness Joining Yours. The Perfection Glows In Every Aspect Of Your Being.

Your Spirit, Your Immortal Soul, Is A Differentiation Of GOD's Spirit. There Is An Entire Universe Of Spiritual Beings, Differentiated From The ONE, GOD, LORD Of All. GOD Is Yet Greater Than All These. This Knowledge Helps You To Understand Your Own Origin. It Also Describes The Destination, Of Your Soul As Reunified With The ONE.

The Reason GOD Differentiates Slivers Of His Being As Independent Spirits Is To Encourage Individual and Diverse Experience Of GOD's Other Creations. The Gift Of Life, Bestowed by GOD Upon You, As Spirit Incarnate in physical being, Allows GOD To Share In the physical universe From Different Perspectives Than GOD's Usual Observation Of His Creations.

Your Soul, Experiencing Conscious Being, Incarnate In this physical universe, Is One Of GOD's Points Of View. Our LORD,

GOD Takes Pleasure Experiencing This World Through Your Consciousness.

You May Experience Any Of The Extraordinary Blessings Of This Sharing. Among these are Boundless Joy, Communion, Forgiveness, Hope, and Love.

You May Experience Spontaneous Seeing, As GOD Joins You To See This Marvelous Creation Through Any or All Of Your Senses. This also includes Your Constructions Of Mind.[5a] This Seeing With You, Is The Pleasure Of GOD. [5b]

You Are Able To See, As You Are The Instrument Of GOD In This World.

This Teacher grew by seeking Enlightenment early in life. A Christian Home may have been an unusual setting To Aspire To Bodhi[5c]. Bodhi Is The Light, Also Known as Enlightenment In Advanced Eastern Religions. There were many distractions along The Way. Yet, In Retrospect, This Way May Have Been The Only Way For Me.

Perfect Knowledge[5d] Grew. Many years were spent learning the sciences and religions. Yet all of this knowledge (learning of facts) did not get me to Enlightenment. Only Acquiring Knowledge (Experience) Through Participation In The Wonderous Occasions Of Life, Elevated My Consciousness. Spiritual Energy Was Becoming More Vigorous In My Soul. My Entire Being Recognized The Movement Of Spiritual Energy In My Body and In My Consciousness. I Discovered That I Could Enhance It. When I Realized That This Energy Continued To Come Directly From GOD, Then The Gateway Opened To Boundless Joy[5e].

Your Spiritual Journey Will Have Its Own Course. You Must Participate To Experience Glory.

# 6

## SEEING WITH THE SENSES

The word "seeing" has many definitions in the English Language. By now You Realize That Our Use Of the Word "Seeing" Is The Spiritual Awareness Of GOD, That Elevates ordinary consciousness To The Appreciation Of GOD In All Things. That is to say that visual sensation transmits visual data from your retina to nerve centers in your brain. You have learned to organize these sensations into meaningful perceptions of Your Mind. Seeing Requires That You Combine a physical perception with The Divine Aspect Of This Reality.

For example, ordinary consciousness recognizes your perception of a waterfall, as a physical view of water falling over a precipice. Ordinary consciousness may not be Moved, other than to notice the event, or to barely notice the event.

However, If You Linger (Stop) and See With GOD, The Magnificence Of The Waterfall Is Experienced. You Are Seeing. You May Not Identify GOD In The Elation You Feel Upon Experiencing The Grandeur Of The Waterfall, but You Are Elevated. You Vividly See The Magnificence of the foaming water as it cascades in free-fall through the air. You Hear The Thundering as the massive wall of water crashes into the pool below. You Feel the cool mist and inhale its richness. You Are Transformed Into The First Heaven, As You Marvel At The Splendid rainbow Before You.

You May or May Not Be Aware That GOD Has Joined Your Consciousness, To Participate In This Glory. It Is The First Heaven – To Have The LORD Join Your Conscious Being, In Any Aspect Of This Life. That Can Be Spontaneous. You May Also Invite GOD To Join You. You, Actively Sharing Your Experience With GOD, Is Truly Glory In This Human Life!

Seeing The Waterfall Is A Divine Event. The waterfall cannot experience this. It has no consciousness. The waterfall is strictly physical reality. It is just water flowing from higher elevation, over physical barriers, to lower elevation.

GOD Created Human Beings So, Through Them, GOD Can Experience His Many Creations, Through Their Eyes. We Call This Sharing, "The Pleasure Of GOD." This Is Your Purpose In Life!

Failure to Share You Experience With GOD, is not a sin. Failure to share your experience with GOD is oblivion. You are oblivious to the Glory possible in your life. You are living as a low consciousness creature, reacting to physical needs and stimuli. It is a shame that our culture entertains this low level of conscious being.

You May Elevate Your Consciousness simply by Pausing To Recognize The Beauty Or Harmony Of Your Surroundings. You May Even Pause (Stop) during an unpleasant experience, To Invite GOD Into Your Consciousness. Then Everything Changes.

Practice Stopping and Seeing[6a]. Your Methods Of Stopping Will Become More Varied. Your Inspiration In Seeing Will Become More Divine.

Seeing, Does Not Just Happen With The sense of sight. Many Humans See Spontaneously With The Sense Of Hearing. Listening

To Inspiring Music Is Seeing With The Ears. Perhaps You Have Put On A Pleasant Tune, or Recall A Song That You Like. You Are Carried Away As You Ride The Music. You Have Stopped And The LORD Has Joined You In This Joy.

Stopping and Seeing In Appreciation Of Music May Be Easier for You than Stopping and Seeing In Appreciation Of A Visual Scene. This Author Is Often Elevated, just driving down the road, As I Listen To My Favorite Tunes.

You May Find The LORD In Your Sense Of Taste. Your Enjoyment Of Delicious Food Will Be Elevated If You Pause To Allow The Flavor Of The Food Or Drink, to Expand In Your Perception.

Yes, Your body is demanding nutrition, so you gobble down mouthfuls, hardly tasting anything, as it passes to your stomach and through your digestive tract. Many eating disorders are motivated by some desire or conditioning that is GOD-forsaken, as The LORD will not join this experience. So-Stop! Allow Each Bite To Carry Flavor To You. GOD Will Be Pleased To Join You.

The sense of smell is less developed in human beings than in some other creatures. It Becomes More Poignant To Pause When You Smell A Pleasant Aroma. This Stopping May Come Easily To You If You Train Yourself To Take A Brief Pause To Appreciate The Rich and Complex Aromas Of Your Flower Garden, The Countryside, or even unpolluted Urban Air.

It Is The Same With Touch. You Feel The Softness Of A Velvet Fabric As Your Fingers Glide Over Its Surface, Pressing Gently To Feel Its Depth.

Seeing Through The Sense Of Touch May Be The Best Aspect Of Your Consciousness To Understand The Second Heaven. In The First Heaven, It Is Just You And GOD Sharing Glory In Your Conscious Experience Of Your Life On earth.

The Second Heaven May Be Introduced in the following manner: Your child stubbed His toe. You Sympathetically Rub the sore spot, gently to Ease the pain. You Console Him As You Feel The Intensity Of His Suffering. You Share This Experience Together. He Is Spiritually Healed By Your Merciful Touch. His physical pain dissipates As You Share This Experience With Him. During this difficult Experience, You Have Stopped, To See His distress. Your Sharing Elevates Both Of You. Yes, The Second Heaven Is The Joining Of Two Individual Spirits, Here In this physical universe. GOD Joins In This Union. When GOD Joins, We Call It Heaven.

This example Is Also A Good One To Introduce The Third Heaven. When You Decided To Mercifully Share With Your Child, To Ease the condition of His stubbed toe, GOD Entered Your Consciousness. You Became The Instrument Of GOD, To Ease His condition.

You are not Perfect, but Perfection Is In You. In Your Righteousness, GOD Will Use You For Divine Purpose. Examine Your Motives. Examine Your Actions. Make Them Pure. Then GOD Will Lead You To Establish Holiness In Your Sphere Of Influence While You Are Incarnate In physical being. This Is The Third Heaven.

Experiences Of The Senses Are Continuous. They Are Present, but Ever Changing. They Become Different Experiences, As You Proceed Through Time, In This Life.

We Have Examined How Stopping and Seeing May Occur In the individual physical senses. Yet Your Consciousness Often Combines Individual sensations Into A Whole Experience. The Best Example May Be The Reciprocating Touch Of Your Beloved, As You Share Each Other's Exciting Aroma, Glimpse Each Other's Beautiful Form and Features, Taste Lovely Lips, Hear The Compliments, Murmurs, and Experience The Thrills Of Romantic Love.

Constructions Of Mind, such as Words Spoken and Thoughts

Shared, Enter The Combination of Conscious Experience. You Are An Advanced Spirit, Differentiated From GOD and Capable Of Divine Consciousness. Your Life Is The Opportunity To Proceed, Living The Glory Of GOD.

# 7

# THE ZEN OF
# WRONG TURNS

## You Made a Mistake.

Oh! I should not be here. Suddenly you realize you have made a
wrong turn. My intended way does not look like this path, you say to
yourself. The geography is unfamiliar. Feelings are not in harmony.
Perhaps you said or did the wrong thing.

Perhaps your career has deviated from your vocation. Perhaps a
Personal Relationship has deteriorated. Your effort is in error. Did I
choose this way, you ask? No, you answer yourself.

Discovering the wrong turn is essential to the way forward. The
tragedy is to be on the wrong path for years. You attempt to make
that path, your path, but it is not.

You are confused. Where am I? How did I get here? You stop in
your tracks, or keep coasting. You are blown by outside forces and
spinning dizzily inside. You are uncertain. You ask yourself, what
do I do next?

## Centering

So - STOP!

Open your senses to safe conduct. Then direct your awareness to that spot at the bottom of your spine. Pivot Easily on your seat to find balance, both body and Soul. Mystics call this Your Base Chakra. In It You Direct location and motion. Be at ease with your current motion. Forget time or urgency or deadlines, or limitations. Allow Stillness To Calm your restlessness.

Take a Deep Breath and release It slowly.

Open Your Consciousness, To See Where You Really Are. Ask Yourself, Why Am I Here, Now? Is it just a wrong turn, or has The LORD Led Me To This?

See The World and Your Position, As GOD Would See It.

Perhaps this is a better place than you had planned. Perhaps the turn avoided catastrophe in a future you will not experience.

See Your Next Choices As GOD Would See Them. Then The Blessing Happens.

> "The LORD shall preserve thee from all evil: he shall preserve thy soul. The LORD shall preserve thy going out and thy coming in from this time forth." (*Holy Bible; Psalm 121: 7-8 KJV*)

Allow Your Conscience, That Is Your Connection Directly To GOD, To Calmly Lead You To The Next Step. Listen To The Still-Small-Voice Of The LORD, In Your Awareness. This is called, "The Leading Of The LORD." Follow That From Your Center, Forward, Using A Better Procedure To A Better Destination.

That may be returning, to find and resume Your originally planned path. It may be a new path Directed From The Center of Your Being.

The Zen[7a] Is The Centering Of Your Consciousness, To See In That Calmness, the wrong turn Is Corrected. You Move Forward Powerfully, With Confidence.

# 8

## CENTERING

A Powerful Centering Technique Is to practice "Stopping." When "Seeing" follows, It will proceed from Your Center. This does not need to originate at a specific Chakra. Rather, Stopping Allows Spiritual Energy, From GOD, To Settle In Your Soul.

> "But you will receive power when the Holy Spirit comes on you; and you will be my witnesses ..."
> *(Holy Bible, Acts 1:8, NIV)*

You might say that The Divine Spiritual Energy "Crystalizes" In Your Soul. It becomes Your Light. You may Circulate Your Light Within Your Soul and Body. You May Project Your Light Upward To GOD or Outward To Other Beings. This Circulation of The Light Is The Most Advanced and Fulfilling Activity Of A Human Being.

A Powerful Meditation Technique Is To Allow Spiritual Energy to Crystalize At Your Center, Flow Up your spine, and Through Crown of your head. Like a bolt of lightning, Your Spiritual Energy Is Received By GOD, and Returned Enhanced In This Worship.

You cannot project Spiritual Energy onto a purely physical object. Unless a physical object has Spirit Incarnated Into It, that object cannot receive or Circulate Spiritual Energy. An example is this cut diamond I just picked out of the jewelry case. It is sparkling, transforming physical light in many patterns. However, this diamond, like all physical reality, has no soul. It does not live and it does not die. Like all our physical universe, it just proceeds through time, controlled by physical forces. It only has Spiritual Significance If You Appreciate it. That Appreciation Is Yours, not power or divinity in the physical diamond.

Human Beings are in need of Spiritual Experience. Humans yearn for It. The sin of idolatry is the attempt to find Spirit in lifeless matter. If You Can View the lifeless object or image, and it Reminds You Of Experience You Share With GOD, then it is a proper symbol for Spirituality. If You worship it as though it were divine, then it is an idol that will diminish Your Spiritual Being.

As artificial intelligence is further developed, it remains an open question as to whether The LORD will Input Spiritual Being into the construct of artificial intelligence, such as, a robot or a computer program. Your body is a physical construct and GOD Incarnated A Soul Into You, so theoretically The LORD Could Imbue Spirit Into a machine.

The opinion of This Author is that only GOD Can Imbue A Part Of GOD's Being Into any physical object. Stated another way, the construct of any artificial intelligence has no soul. As soon as the physical power to its mechanism, is turned off, that artificial intelligence ceases to exist.

Note that if the artificial intelligence initiated action, those causes and effects may continue to operate in reality, during and after the ceasing of the artificial intelligence. Though causality continues to operate in both physical and Spiritual Reality, the Subject is different. Your Immortal Soul Is The Subject Of Your Spiritual Being. Your

Soul Continues In Our Spiritual Universe, After your physical death. There is no subject, identity, or awareness in an artificial Intelligence mechanism that continues after that mechanism ceases to function. Do not diminish Your Immortal Soul by treating Yourself as merely a physical object.

Centering Is An Effort Of The Consciousness Of The Individual Spirit, Incarnate In a physical body. Centering Enables Stopping and Seeing. Various Religious Traditions May Name Stopping as, Emptiness, Stopping The World, Clearing The Mind, or Other Disciplines to Focus Consciousness on nothing. Then The CLEAR LIGHT Of GOD, Will Fill the void.

When You Meditate to achieve "emptiness" or "nothingness", long enough, You Will Realize That "nothingness" does not exist. Only GOD, The CLEAR LIGHT, Exists, Before, During, and After, Everything.

There Is no emptiness. There Is, Only THE CLEAR LIGHT. SEE That.

# 9

## TURNING THE LIGHT AROUND

Have you ever had some time off your regular job and went to a new place? Upon arrival Everything Seemed New and Wonderful. You Felt A Surge Of Joy and Excitement. Perhaps You Were walking in the woods and suddenly came upon a waterfall. Your World Stopped, Except For Beholding The Magnificence Of The Waterfall. Perhaps You Were At A Concert and Were Swept Away By The Lovely Music.

In Those Moments GOD Was With You. Your Spontaneous Expanded Sense Of Awareness Was GOD Sharing With You. This was Enlightenment. You Became Immortal In Those Moments. The Next Step In Your Spiritual Journey Is For You To Become Aware Of This. To Seek It. To Find It.

When Your Spirit Sees and Welcomes The LORD To Share With You, You Are "Turning The Light Around." [8a]

This Advanced Worship Is About The Movement Of Spiritual Energy. Spiritual Energy Is The LIGHT. It is Divine. Spiritual Energy Is Of The Essence Of GOD.

Enlightenment Starts By Opening Your Consciousness. Turning The Light Around Means, Receiving The Light Of GOD, Then Turning It Around In Your Soul To Become ONE With GOD.

"If you do practice for a single breath, then you are a realized immortal for a breath." (*Thomas Cleary, The Secret of the Golden Flower, p. 64. [HarperCollins, 1991]*)

In This Manner, Life Is Fulfilled As You Live it.

# 10

## CIRCULATING THE LIGHT

The Occasions Of Your Sharing The Light Of GOD, With GOD, Will Become More Frequent As You Set Aside mundane matters of this human Life.

Your Soul Swells With Spiritual Energy. Your Light Grows As You Share It Back To GOD. You Have Enhanced The Light As You Turn It In Your Soul. GOD Is Very Pleased As The LORD Receives Your Light Back Into The ONE.

Open Your Soul. GOD will Share The Light Back To You, Further Enhanced. Receive It, and Turn The Light Around, Again In Your Soul.

This Is One Spiritual Oscillation. With Each Cycle, Spritual Energy Increases. The Light Is Glorious As It Increases, Shared By Spiritual Beings. This Is Called "Circulating The Light" [9a].

You May Become The Instrument Of GOD. Through You, GOD May Share The Light With Other Human Beings. You Can Choose To Project The Light In One Or Many Ways, Causing Another Person to Become Elevated By Your Luminous Communication. The LORD Is Always Present In Your Projection Of Spiritual Energy.

Consider Motherhood. Through The Joy With A Loving Man, You Have Become With Child. The LORD Has Bestowed Upon You The Magnificent Fusion Of A Spirit Into A New Human Being. Perhaps It Is More Accurate To Describe The Incarnation As, The Spiritual Being Of Your Child Chose To Become Alive With You. This Is One Aspect Of GOD Participating With You.

Consider Mercy. Instead of viewing an unfortunate Person with distain or apathy, Share The Light Of Love Through Mercy To That Person. Whether Your Mercy Is A Prayer For Their Well-Being, or Lending A Hand To Improve Their Condition, Share Divine Energy With That Person. The LORD Moves To That Person Through Your Mercy.

If You Expand Mercy, Beyond Justice, to Share The Mercy Of GOD With A Being Who has done you wrong, That Is Forgiveness. Your Light Becomes Brilliant, In Forgiveness. The LORD Is Very Pleased.

Indeed, Through You GOD May Share The Light With Any Spiritual Being. Your Traditions May Be Different Than Mine, but I Share The Divine Light With You and Any Spiritual Being That Can Share This Light Of Love.

You May, In Turn, STOP. Open Your Soul To SEE The Perfection Of This Situation, As The LORD SEE's It Though You. In The Fullness Of This Consciousness, You May Circulate The Light Of GOD With All Beings.

GOD Bless You[9b].

# 11

## RESEARCH NOTES, CREDITS, AND EXPANSIONS

[1a] It is Attained: gained or acquired; especially through merit or as a result of effort or action. (*www.vocabulary.com*)

["Stopping and Seeing" Is Revealed As An Advanced Worship Technique By which The Individual Spirit, Incarnate, May Welcome The LORD, GOD, Into Its Consciousness, To Participate, In The Wonderous Experience Of This Life Through The physical senses.

More Broadly, "Stopping and Seeing" May Reunite The Individual Spirit With GOD In Spiritual Reality, Beyond this physical universe. Of Course, This "Seeing" is Spiritual "Seeing", Relating As A Divine Being to the physical universe, or what can be Observed in physical reality.

Whether "Seeing" Is Shared With GOD by Your Spirit, Incarnate In Your physical Being, or Shared As You Approach GOD In Spiritual Being, Beyond This Life, "The Light" is not photon light, or the electromagnetic energy stimulating any of

Your senses (sight, sound, touch, taste, or smell). It is Spiritual LIGHT, Which Is GOD. This is Spiritual Enlightenment.]

[1b] I AM: "And God said unto Moses, I AM THAT I AM: and he said, Thus shalt thou say unto the children of Israel, I AM hath sent me unto you." (*Holy Bible; Exodus 3:14 KJV*); capital letters added for emphasis.

[The Primary Awareness Of My Human Consciousness It That "I Am". It is the first-person case of the verb "to be". It is fundamental to each human experience. Our conclusion is that Each Person Knowing That "I Am", Proves The Identity Of The Spiritual Self, GOD's Presence In Each Of Us. It Is A Sliver Of The Great "I AM", That Is GOD.]

[2a] STOP: To cease; to no longer continue (*en.wikipedia.org*)

[2b] Peace, Be Still!: "And he [Jesus] arose, and rebuked the wind, and said unto the sea, Peace, be still. And the wind ceased, and there was a great calm." (*Holy Bible, Mark 4:39 KJV*)

*[Stopping and Seeing* Reveals The Expanded Meaning Of Jesus Command. Not only Does The WORD Made Flesh In The Person Of JESUS CHRIST Operate To Command physical forces, controlling physical reality, but JESUS Commands Your Stormy Mind To Stop, and Be Still. Then The LORD Enters Your Consciousness As You "See" With Divine Consciousness.]

Below are some other Techniques For Stopping:

<u>Be Still:</u> Songs such as *Still, Still, Still* (Austrian Christmas Song; Georg Gotsch lyrics), will lull you to Stop and set aside the single

mindedness of goal-oriented consciousness. There is a time and purpose for concentrated effort toward earthly goals. In fact, once You Stop, and learn to See, Seeing, during your everyday endeavors will keep you Centered Spiritually. Then you can Live In The Kingdom Of GOD, right here on earth.

Quietude: Attain The State Of Quietude by Interrupting the chatter in Your Mind. Stop, by Force Of Will, to silence the ordinary flow of Consciousness. Open Your Senses. In That Silence You Will "See".

Breathwork: If you concentrate on rhythmic breathing, it is called "Breathwork". To concentrate on breathing, you will Stop the incessant chatter in your mind. Breathwork allows you to "Center" and "Purify" Your Spirit. Then You Can See.

There are many Breathwork techniques. If You Feel lost, disoriented, or anxious, I recommend slow, deep, belly-breathing. Begin each breath inhaling in Your lower belly. As your lower lungs fill, bring incoming breath upward in front of your heart, then up to your throat in your upper lungs. Hold your lungs full of air for a moment, then exhale naturally as you relax. This is the time to Focus Your Mind On Welcoming The LORD Into Your Consciousness, To See The Perfection Of All Around You.

Be Here Now! Babba Ram Das published his famous book by that name, *(Be Here Now; Lama Foundation. ISBN 0-517-54305-2)*, to lead You to Center Yourself, In The Present. Thoughts of the past and plans for the future distract Your Consciousness away from The Perfection Of This Moment. When You Open all Your Senses To Be At ONE With The Fullness Of The Present, GOD

Joins You To See It Through Your Consciousness, Right-Here, Right-Now.

A Good Cry: Crying is a natural release of Spiritual tension. Crying Stops the crescendo of cares that overburden Your Soul. Allow Yourself To Emerge from the sorrow, To See Reality As It Really Is.

Tears of Joy are Seeing, as you are overwhelmed by the Perfection as GOD Joins Your Experience.

Be Empty: Emptiness is often portrayed as the goal of Buddhist Meditations. Emptiness is not the goal. Seeking emptiness Is The First Step Toward Fulfillment.

The following excerpt from *GOD – The Dimensional Revelation* Guides You From Ordinary Consciousness, To emptiness. In apparent emptiness, You Are Filled With THE CLEAR LIGHT, Which Is GOD.

"The yin-yang (i.e., taijitu) shows a balance between two opposites, with a portion of the opposite element in each section. In Taoist metaphysics, distinctions between good and bad, along with other dichotomous moral judgments, are perceptual, not real; so, the duality of yin and yang is an indivisible whole." (*en.wikipedia.org*)

(*https://en.wikipedia.org/wiki/Taijitu#/media/File:Yin_yang.svg*)

[*GOD - The Dimensional Revelation*, Notes That The Balance Depicted In The Taijitu Symbol Can Be A Harmonious Coexistence Of The Opposites, the harmonious interplay of opposite pairs.

It also represents the conflict of the opposites when harmony breaks down.

Our Teaching Recalls The Buddhist Meditation Seeking emptiness of mind, Represented by the "empty" circle. This Principle is often confused by a criticism of "emptiness," as "no god." As You Approach "emptiness, You Will See -

**There is no emptiness. There is no void. There is only The CLEAR LIGHT.** Emptiness is the void that cannot exist, so You cannot attain emptiness. All, Remains Filled With The CLEAR LIGHT.

Be Enlightened In The True GOD, Our 10th Dimension Spiritual and Our Seventh Heaven. The "conflict of the opposites" disappears Upon Reunification With The LORD.

Our Teaching Appreciates The Purity Of The White Void. We Join With GOD As The CLEAR LIGHT Of The Void.]

Drawing of the physically white "emptiness," representing Pure Spirit, THE CLEAR LIGHT Of the void.
*Illustration by Allyn Richert AD 2022.*

*Mik Ulyannikov/Shutterstock 44621095,*
*edited by Allyn Richert AD 2022*

[The Journey of a Soul, Differentiated From the ONE, through many different manifestations until ultimate Reunification with GOD, May be experienced in many different ways. Indeed, The Journey Of Your Soul may be vastly different from the Journey of Another Soul or Spirit. The three illustrations above, from the Harmony or conflict of the opposites, to appear empty, yet Gloriously Enlightened In Union With The CLEAR LIGHT, Is One Journey Your Soul May Take.

During This Human Life, Your Spiritual Journey May Be Fulfilled Through Your Meditative Experience Of Love In Harmonizing The Opposites as shown in the Taijitu Symbol. One Way To Reunify With The LORD, Is To Stop the incessant background chatter in Consciousness. The Stopping as represented by the Empty Circle. This void in Consciousness Is Filled With The CLEAR LIGHT Of GOD, As You SEE The Perfection, With Any And All Of Your Senses. This Is Represented By the Illustration Of Brilliant Light.] (*expanded quotations from GOD-The Dimensional Revelation, p.390-391, Allyn Richert 2023)*

[3a] GOD Is In You:

Jesus Said, "At that day you will know that I am in My Father, and you in Me, and I in you." (*Holy Bible, John 14:19 NKJV*)

[3b] Welcome GOD Into Your Consciousness:

"Jesus answered him, If anyone loves me, he will keep my word, and my Father will love him, and we will come to him and make our home with him." (*Holy Bible, John 14:23 NKJV*)

[5a] Constructions Of Mind:

A materialist may say that, "everything is a construct of the mind" just means that all you sense/imagine is an interpretation of the 'real' world via sense data (and your memories of sense data) by your brain. And your brain is made of squishy biological bits and neurons that are capable of coding and interpreting such sense data."

We argue for a reformulation of Theory of Mind (ToM) through a systematic two-stage approach, beginning with a deconstruction of the construct into a comprehensive set of basic component processes, followed by a complementary reconstruction from which a scientifically tractable concept of ToM can be recovered. (*Deconstructing and Reconstructing Theory Of Mind; 2014; Sara M. Schaafsma; Donald W. Pfaff;robert P. Spunt; Ralph Adolphs*)

Cosmologically, a 3-dimensional object is a primary unit of being in our physical universe. An object is not a construct of Mind. It exists independently of the Observer. (*GOD – The Dimensional Revelation, p.84, Allyn Richert, 2023*)

*GOD-The Dimensional Revelation* Resolves mind-brain duality, the "hard problem" of consciousness (*David Chalmers*), By Revealing That The "problem" Is Self-imposed by a materialistic point of view. The Individual Spirit Is A Component Of "Mind" That Makes Mind Non-physical. Your Individual Spirit Is Fused During Your Lifetime With Your brain and general physiology.

(*GOD-The Dimensional Revelation, p.199, Allyn Richert, 2023*). [*Stopping And Seeing* Reemphasizes that Your Mind is a Fusion of Your physical brain processes with Your Spirit, To Create Your Reality In This Life. Constructs Of Mind Proceed With both physical and Spiritual Processes. Theory of Mind, must include both for Mind to exist.]

[5b] The Pleasure Of GOD:

"[*GOD - The Dimensional Revelation*, Reveals, that GOD Created the physical universe for His Pleasure. The Pleasure of GOD is not hedonistic pleasure. Rather GOD Is Pleased By Observing and Participating In Various Of GOD's Creations. Recognizing that material being is barren, GOD Created Life With Individual Consciousness. GOD Did This By Instructing Individual Spirits Of The Spiritual Universe To Penetrate the boundaries of physical being and Merge With matter To Manifest Creatures Of Life on Earth. The Nature Of Spiritual Being Is That It Has The Potential Of God-Consciousness. That Is, GOD May Choose To Re-Enter His Creation Through Your Consciousness and Participate In Our Unique and Wonderful Reality.]"
*(GOD-The Dimensional Revelation, p.267, Allyn Richert, 2023)*

"for I am God, and there is none else... My counsel shall stand, and I will do all my pleasure." (*Holy Bible, Isaiah 46:9,10 KJV*)

"The LORD does whatever pleases him, in the heavens and on the earth, in the seas and all their depths." *(Holy Bible, Psalm 135:6 NIV)*

"[We live in a manifestation of the Divine. Each of our sensations, experiences, actions, and accomplishments are the manifestations of GOD in our reality. Each Human Being has consciousness. That consciousness is the awareness of GOD in this reality. Divine Experience of those manifestations is "The Pleasure of GOD". Let us be sure that GOD is well pleased by each of our Beings, in this manifestation.]" (*The Pleasure of GOD p.2, Allyn Richert, 2016*)

[5c] Bodhi:

The Conscious State Of Bodhi Is Being In Nirvana. In Hinduism Samsara is the worldly state of being in this Life. Nirvana is attained by The Pure In Spirit, In The Next Life.

Some sects of Buddhism Hold That Both Samsara and Nirvana Are Attained By A Being, even in This Life on earth. *Stopping and Seeing*, Affirms That When You Stop and See, You Are In Nirvana As GOD Shares Your Consciousness. You Are briefly Reunited With The ONE. GOD Is Very Pleased, As You Share This State Of Being.

[5d] Perfect Knowledge:

"so that you may live a life worthy of the Lord and please him in every way: bearing fruit in every good work, growing in the knowledge of God," (*Holy Bible, Colossians 1:10 NIV*)

"Understanding the dynamic operation between the material and the Spiritual is called "Perfect Knowledge" by philosophers. In religion it is called "Wisdom"." (*The Creator's Creed, p.4, Allyn Richert, 2015*)

[5c] Boundless Joy:

The Maitri Upanishad teaches that peace begins in one's own mind, in one's longing for truth, in looking within, and that "a quietness of mind overcomes good and evil works, and in quietness the soul is one: then one feels the joy of eternity." (*Juan Mascaró; The Upanishads. Penguin. pp. 103–104. 1965*)

"Your heart now fully awakens. You experience Divine and Unity Consciousness.

There is no longer any separation. No giver, given, or giving. No sense of "I" or "me," just an awareness of Oneness. You still live "in the world," but are no longer "of the world."

Your spiritual practice is Pure Joy. All the chakras are open, spiritual energy flows freely." (*https://chopra.com/articles/the-7-stages-of-spiritual-development; Roger Gabriel December 6, 2018)*

[6a] Stopping and Seeing:

"…before you continuously practice stopping and continue it by seeing, practice seeing and continue it by stopping. This is the twin cultivation of stopping and seeing. This is turning the light around. The turning around is stopping, the light is seeing. Stopping without seeing is called turning around without light; seeing without stopping is called having light without turning it around. Remember this." *The Secret of the Golden Flower 3:17-18, Thomas Cleary translation 1991, HarperCollins*

"If you do practice for a single breath, then you are a realized immortal for a breath…" (*The Secret of the Golden Flower 13; p 64 trans. Thomas Cleary (HarperCollins, 1991)*

[7a] Zen: "Chán points directly to the human mind, to enable people to see their true nature and become buddhas." (*Nan, Huai-Chin. Basic Buddhism: Exploring Buddhism and Zen. 1997. p. 92)*

[8a] Turning The Light Around.:

"The golden flower is light. . . The celestial mind is like a house; the light is the master of the house. Therefore, once you turn the light around, the energies throughout the body all rise. Just turn the light around; this is the unexcelled truth."… "Turning the light around is the secret of dissolving darkness and controlling the lower soul. There is no exercise to restore 'the creative", only the secret of turning the light around. The light itself is 'the creative;' to turn it around is to restore it." (*Secret of the Golden Flower, pp. 10, 11, 15; Thomas Cleary translation 1991, HarperCollins*)

"Turning the light around is not turning around the light of one body, but turning around the very energy of Creation" (*The Secret of the Golden Flower 3:5; Thomas Cleary translation 1991, HarperCollins*)

"People experience higher things individually, according to their faculties and capacities...it is necessary for you to attain faith on your own. Only then is the true primal unified energy present." (*The Secret of the Golden Flower 6:10, 11; Thomas Cleary translation 1991, HarperCollins*)

"With each level of progress in practice, the efflorescence of the light increases in magnitude, and the method of turning around becomes subtler. Previously one controlled the inside from the outside; now one abides in the center and controls the outside."

*(The Secret of the Golden Flower 8:7; Thomas Cleary translation 1991, HarperCollins)*

"Understanding This Is Not Enough. Turning The Light Around Must Be Experienced Through Participation.

Our Teaching also Welcomes You To Share The Light Of Love At Any Stage Of Your Spiritual Development. You need not Be A Master To Exchange Spiritual Energy With Another Spirit."
*(GOD-The Dimensional Revelation, p.383, Allyn Richert 2023)*

"The method of turning the light around basically is to be carried on whether walking, standing, sitting, or reclining. It is only essential that you yourself find the opening of potential." (*The Secret of the*

*Golden Flower, Chapter 10; p 51; Thomas Cleary translation 1991, HarperCollins)*

[9a] Circulating The Light:

"[*GOD - The Dimensional Revelation* Reveals That The Exchange Of Spiritual Energy With GOD Is An Oscillating Exchange. The Light Is Given To You By GOD. You Circulate The Light In Your Center. The Light Increases As You Appreciate It. Through Prayer, Meditation, and Worship, You Share The Light Back With GOD. GOD Appreciates The Light You Share. GOD Returns It To You, Enhanced. Spiritual Energy Increases With Each Cycle. This Oscillation Is The Basis For Spiritual Enlightenment.

This Exchange Is Often interrupted During A Human Life To Attend biological needs. There are other distractions.

When You Have Mastered Turning The Light At Your Center, Then You Can Turn The Light Around To Project It Outwardly To Other Living Beings. Sharing The Light Broadens The Oscillation and Circulation Of The Light. This Unifies and Elevates Spirit. GOD Is Very Pleased and You Are Fulfilled.]" (*GOD-The Dimensional Revelation, p.336, Allyn Richert 2023*)

Master Lu-Tsu said, Where there is a gradual success in producing the circulation of the light, a man must not give up his ordinary occupation in doing it. (*The Secret of the Golden Flower, Richard Wilhelm translation 1929; Translated into English by Cary F. Baynes 1962; Chapter 7, p.51*)

[9b] GOD Bless You:

> The LORD bless you and keep you;
> The Lord make His face shine upon you, And be gracious to you;
> The Lord lift up His countenance upon you, And give you peace.
> *(Holy Bible, Numbers 6:24–26 NKJV)*

Printed in the United States
by Baker & Taylor Publisher Services